WRITTEN BY
TONY BRADMAN

ILLUSTRATED BY
JONATRONIX

CHASING BIRDY

Contents

The micro-friends 2
Chapter 1: The new girl 3
Chapter 2: Time shift 12
Chapter 3: The Tick-Tock Man 18
Chapter 4: The Artefacts of Time 25
About Leonardo da Vinci 32

OXFORD
UNIVERSITY PRESS

The micro-friends

Max, Cat, Ant and Tiger are four ordinary children with four extraordinary watches. When activated, their watches allow them to shrink to micro-size.

To shrink: turn the dial anticlockwise, then press the X. To grow, reverse the process.

- hologram communicator
- magni-scope
- flip up camera
- warning light
- tracking device
- internet access
- torch

Chapter 1: The new girl

It was just a normal school day …

"Max, what's the answer to question ten?"

"Ssshhh! I'm trying to concentrate!"

The classroom door opened. All eyes turned to look at the new girl …

"Say hello to your new classmate, everyone."

"Birdy, you can sit with Cat. She'll look after you."

"Hi, Birdy! Welcome to our class."

Birdy ignored Cat.

Charming!

3

Later that day, at the end of school …

I tried to talk to her but she's ignored me all day.

Maybe she's shy.

What's she got in that bag?

Tiger glanced down at his watch.

Look! The danger signal!

What set it off?

It can't have been Birdy … can it?

I think we'd better try to find out.

At last, the storm I've been waiting for!

RUMBLE, RUMBLE, RUMBLE

Max and the others tried to keep Birdy in sight as she hurried through the streets of Greenville.

"Why's she in such a rush?"

"Maybe her library books are overdue."

"Where is she? I can't see her!"

"There!"

It looked as if Birdy was going right to the top of the building, but there was only one lift!

"Let's take the stairs!"

"Hurry up, everyone!"

TO THE CLOCK TOWER
Are we at the top yet?
Come on, slowcoach!
TO THE CLOCK TOWER
Wait, maybe we should … you know … just in case.
Good idea, Max!
After three, guys. One, two, three …

They cautiously made their way round the walkway.
Look!
Sssshhhhh!
RUMBLE, CRACKLE, RUMBLE
Cool outfit.
What's she doing now?
I don't know …

"What is that thing?"

"I think we're about to find out!"

CRACKLE, CRACKLE

As lightning struck ... it seemed as if the machine came to life.

ZAP! POW!

HUMMMMMM ...

"Huh? My watch is going crazy."

Time to go …

It's dragging us in!

AAAAARRRRRGGGHHH!

I've got you, Ant!

I can't hold on …

Chapter 2: Time shift

"I … can't … take … much … more … of … this!"

Just then, Max thought he saw an opening ahead.

"Oww!"

"Ouch!"

Whoa, that was intense.
Everyone OK?
I think so, but where are we?
No idea. We could be anywhere.
Let's go back to normal size and find out.
Well, I don't think we're in Greenville any more.
Looks like we might be stuck here for the time being.
POP!
Up ahead in the alley …
What are you lot doing here? How did you get through the Escape Wheel?

Birdy slid her hand into a metal glove.

We should be asking the questions, not you.

Yes, who are you?

I don't have time for this. Tell me who you really are and how you got here ... or else.

CLICK ... BZZZZZ ... CRACKLE ...

Hey, take it easy! We don't know how we got here ourselves.

Actually, I believe I've worked that out. It's because of our watches ...

... I think that vortex you created somehow locked on to them and activated the time-shift mode.

Let me see that watch! This technology is very advanced. Where did you get it?
Hey!
We need some answers first. Like, where are we?
And WHEN?
You're in Italy. 15th-century Florence to be precise.
TICK-TOCK, TICK-TOCK, TICK-TOCK
Can anyone else hear that?
TICK-TOCK!
Get out of here! Go back to your own time before you get hurt!

I'm not going anywhere until we find out what's going on.
Me neither.
We're losing her, she's on the other side of the square!
She's gone!
Then, Cat had an idea …
Birdy's Escape Wheel gave off a lot of energy. Maybe I can track it.
She's heading north!
?!?!?

Cat's watch gave some worrying readings.

I don't understand … She doesn't seem to be on the ground any more.

Er … I think we have visual contact.

Now that really IS cool.

So that's why she's called Birdy!

Chapter 3: The Tick-Tock Man

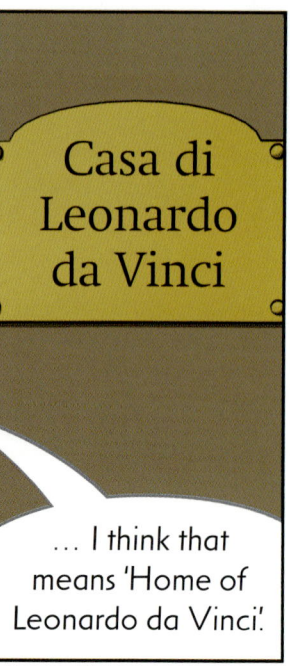

"She's inside this house."

"Why this house? Who do you think lives here?"

"There's your answer …"

Casa di Leonardo da Vinci

"… I think that means 'Home of Leonardo da Vinci'."

"Isn't he kind of famous?"

"*Kind of*? He's only one of the most famous artists and inventors of all time."

"So what's Birdy doing here?"

"Only one way to find out."

TICK-TOCK …
TICK-TOCK …
TICK-TOCK

18

TICK-TOCK ...
TICK-TOCK ...
TICK-TOCK

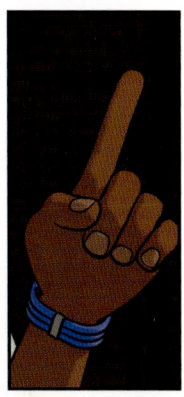

TICK-TOCK ...
TICK-TOCK ...
TICK-TOCK

CRASH!
SMASH!
CRASH!

It's him again! Who is he?

Don't you mean WHAT is he?

The figure appeared to be some kind of robot!

The micro-friends knew they had to help Birdy.

I'll untie her feet. Tiger, you untie her hands. Ant, keep an eye on that thing. Cat, let Birdy know what's going on.

"Psst! We're here to help. You'll be free soon."

Max and Tiger quickly loosened the knots of the ropes.

"Let's get out of here!"

"Mission accomplished. Returning to base …"

"Stop!"

"Aaarrgggh!"

TICK-TOCK-TICK-TOCK-TICK-TOCK…

ZAP! CRACKLE! POW!

SLAM! CRACKLE! BUZZ!

You won't get away!

Are you OK, Cat?

I'm fine ... I think.

Let's get back to normal size.

You'd better tell us what's going on, Birdy.

I REALLY don't have time for this!

Hey, we did just save you from that robot.

OK, you did save me from the Tick-Tock Man, and thanks. But I still have to save the world. So stand back …

Birdy made some adjustments to her metal glove.

KERRRPOW!

I really have to get one of those.

Not again!

23

Preparing to time jump. Increasing energy level.

Jumping ... now.

CRACKLE!

WHHOOOOSSSSH! ZAP! HUMMMMMM ...

24

Chapter 4: The Artefacts of Time

The friends wanted answers …

Nooooo!

OK, Birdy, start talking.

I can't. I don't have –

– Time?

No. I don't. I have to get after him!

Just wait a second. We might be able to help you.

Help me? What are you talking about?

You mentioned saving the world … We've got a bit of experience with that kind of thing.

But we need to know what we're getting into.

OK. You really want to know?

I'm from the future.

Birdy

Birdy's **backpack** holds all of her time-travelling kit … plus all her snacks!

Birdy's **pocket watch** tells her which year she is in. It also helps her to track and locate Tick-Tock Men. Oh, and it tells the time, too!

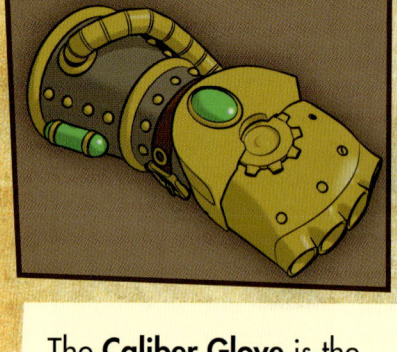

The **Caliber Glove** is the only effective weapon against the Tick-Tock Men. It holds a number of cartridges which contain magnetic coated quartz discs or *cogs*. When a cog hits a Tick-Tock Man in the right spot – an exposed bit of machinery on the back of the robot's neck – it forces them to wind down.

Birdy uses the **Escape Wheel** to travel through time. It requires a large amount of energy to get the vortex to work, such as a lightning strike.

Pit Stopping

Birdy's Escape Wheel is considered to be 'old-tech' where she comes from. It was a prototype designed by her gran, an important scientist. The wheel doesn't always work that well, which was why she ended up meeting Max, Cat, Ant and Tiger. The storm that created the vortex wasn't powerful enough to get her all the way back to 15th-century Florence, so she had to 'Pit Stop' in Greenville. Stuck there, she had to wait for a new storm strong enough to get her all the way back in time to her proper destination.

The future?

Yes. I'm from 2099. In seven days – in my time – an asteroid will hit Earth. Everything will be wiped out.

I still don't understand … What's that got to do with you chasing a weird robot round 15th-century Florence?

That Tick-Tock Man, and others like it, have been sent back from the future to collect seven special Artefacts of Time.

And they've just got the first one – a design for a water clock – one of the cleverest things Leonardo da Vinci ever invented.

Who would want an old design?

27

A man called Kalvin Spearhead wants to use the Artefacts to build a powerful vortex machine.

He says that if he creates a big enough vortex, he'll be able to send lots of people back in time and save them from the asteroid.

Sounds like you don't trust this Spearhead guy?

No, I don't. My gran and I have seen his plans for the machine –

Your gran?

Gran's the head scientist at Spearhead's company.

Spearhead's machine will never be able to transport the amount of people he's talking about.

So you don't think he's telling the truth?

No. Even if he is, sending that amount of people back in time will have a devastating effect on history!

What about the asteroid?

My gran is working on another plan for that.

Meanwhile, you've come back in time to stop the Tick-Tock Men?

Yes.

28

"That's a lot to handle all on your own."

"I know."

"So maybe you could do with some help?"

"Maybe I could."

"Are you ready?"

Meanwhile … Leonardo finally made it home.

I've been robbed!

Ummm, not much missing, though. Only a sketch for an old idea … Good job I made a copy.

The things Leonardo had seen that day had given him lots of new ideas, too!

Leonardo da Vinci was born on 15th April 1452 in Vinci – a town near Florence in Italy. Therefore, his name actually means 'Leonardo from Vinci'.

Leonardo was an artist, sculptor, engineer, architect, scientist and inventor … in fact, he was an all-round genius! He studied human and animal anatomy to help him with his painting and sculpture.

The Mona Lisa is his best-known work of art – and one of the most famous paintings in the world. It is thought that the portrait is of a woman called Lisa Gherardini – a lady from Florence – but it's her mysterious smile that has made it famous. The painting is in the Louvre art gallery in Paris.

Leonardo made designs for all sorts of amazing machines, including a bicycle, a tank, and a submarine, although none of them were ever built. He designed lots of clocks, including an alarm clock that was powered by water. He was very interested in flight too, and designed an aeroplane, an 'ornithopter' – a plane with wings like a bird!

Leonardo died on 2nd May 1519 in France. He was aged 67. When he died, he left 13 000 pages of notes and diagrams full of ideas and inventions.